NATIONAL GEOGRAPHIC

Worlds of Opportunity

PATHFINDER EDITION

By Bonnie Brook

T0308178

CONTENTS

KAKENYA'S DREAM
A Future of Hope

By Bonnie Brook

These women walk along the road that leads to Kakenya's village in Kenya.

Most explorers go somewhere far from home to make their discoveries. National Geographic Emerging Explorer Kakenya Ntaiya has come home to Kenya to make her dream of opportunity come true.

In 2000, one girl in the small Maasai village of Enoosaen, Kenya, had a different plan. She wanted to continue her education—to go on from secondary school to college in the United States. In return, she promised to use her education to benefit the people of Enoosaen.

She urged her parents and the village elders to let her go. It was the start of fulfilling one girl's dream. It was how that girl, Kakenya Ntaiya, became part of a global **migration**.

Today, more than 3 percent of the world's population—more than 200 million people—live outside their country of birth. Millions more have moved or been moved within their home borders. Much of this movement is caused by economic pressures. Some is forced by damage to the environment or by human conflict. Some migrations spring from opportunities far from home.

One thing is for certain: people are on the move like never before. Who are these people on the move? Where are they going? How will they change society? Most importantly, how will their journey change who they are?

This Maasai boy herds cows outside his village in Kenya.

A village elder blesses Kakenya's family at their home in Enoosaen.

Kakenya's Dream

Like others before her, Kakenya Ntaiya came to the United States seeking the opportunity to build a better future for herself and others. Unlike **refugees** who are forced to leave home to find safety from war, persecution, or other hardships, Kakenya did not *have to* migrate, or leave home. It was Kakenya's choice to go to college in the United States. Hers was a **voluntary** migration. In fact, she had to convince her parents and the village elders to let her go.

To the people of Enoosaen, life in the United States was hard to imagine. In Enoosaen, houses are made of mud-bricks. Cows and chickens wander around the village. There is no running water or electricity, and the closest paved road is many miles away. Most importantly, the girls of Enoosaen do not go beyond the fields of corn and sugar cane that surround the small village. Why would a girl want to travel so far away? Still, Kakenya, the eldest of eight children, was set on coming to America.

A Girl Will Never Forget Her Home

Kakenya was stubborn and persistent. She convinced her parents that she deserved the opportunity to study in the United States. She also promised the village elders that she would give back for all they had given her. Kakenya vowed to come back to her village and build a school for girls. She would share the knowledge she gained in the United States. She would use it to give young girls in her region the opportunity to receive a quality education.

"A girl will never forget her home," the elders said. They believed that Kakenya would remember her ties to the village and return. They knew that she had already won a **scholarship** from Randolph-Macon Woman's College in the United States. But Kakenya's own efforts were not enough to pay her way. So, the entire village collected money to pay for her journey. With their blessings, Kakenya set off for Lynchburg, Virginia, to fulfill her hopes for her village.

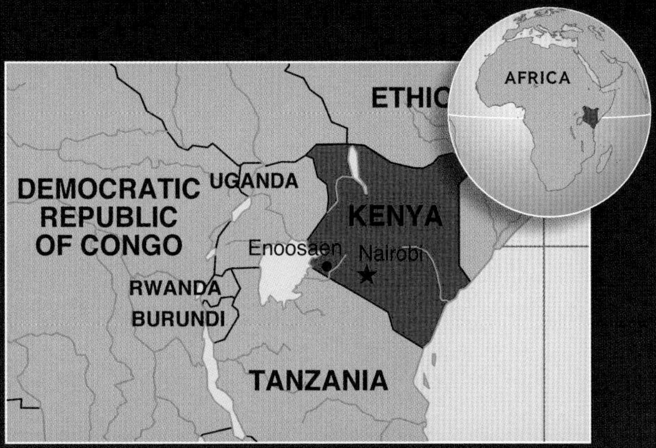

Kakenya gets a hug from a friend in the college cafeteria.

Life in a New Culture

Once she arrived at Randolph-Macon Woman's College, there was much for Kakenya to absorb about life in America. In addition to her freshman studies, there were first-time experiences with plumbing, silverware, superstores, and even snow. Friends volunteered to be the first to take Kakenya to a movie or a fast-food restaurant.

Fortunately, other international students shared the classrooms at Randolph-Macon with Kakenya. They had also come to America for the opportunity to gain valuable knowledge. Kakenya could relate to their experiences.

Kakenya knew she had to make the most of her time in the United States. During her time at Randolph-Macon, she worked in a computer lab to earn extra money.

She also traveled for mock African Union conferences to New York and Washington, D.C. Each day, Kakenya gave thanks to the people from home who made this possible for her.

Promises to Keep

During this time, Kakenya was often overwhelmed by the tasks before her. Not only did she have to complete her studies successfully, she also had debts to pay to her village. She had a school for girls to build. When things were toughest, Kakenya turned to her school friends, knowing they would understand. This always helped her keep going.

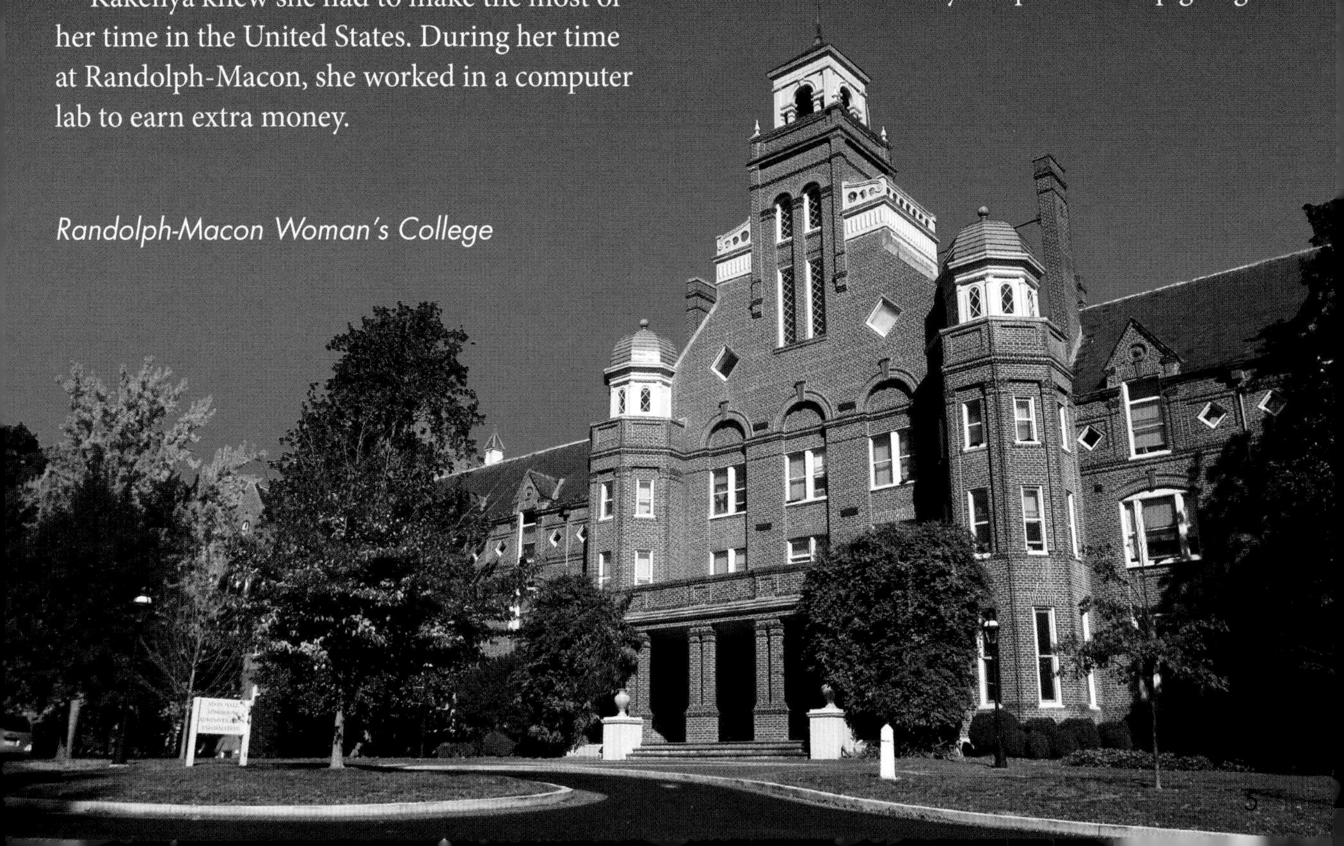

Randolph-Macon Woman's College

Kakenya reads with fourth-grade girls from her school in Enoosaen.

Promises Kept

After receiving her undergraduate degree, Kakenya went on to study for a doctorate in education from the University of Pittsburgh. Then she returned home to Enoosaen.

"Today, I am working to fulfill the promise I made years ago: to return to my village and give back," Kakenya says. "Since 2006, I have been working to build a girls' school in Enoosaen so that other young African girls might travel the same path I did—to education, self-realization, and leadership. This is my dream."

Kakenya is working hard to achieve her dream. Her school for girls, the Kakenya Center for Excellence, opened in May 2009 with 32 fourth-grade students. In January 2010, the center enrolled an additional 31 students. The plan is to enroll 150 students in grades four through eight by 2013.

Academics and Leadership

Each grade has its own classroom at the school. The girls learn English, Swahili, math, science, geography, history, religion, the arts, and physical education. A leadership training program gives girls firsthand experience in running student councils, extracurricular activities, and community outreach programs.

Kakenya wants the girls at her school to use their experiences to build confidence. She believes that "personal involvement promotes self-confidence." She continues, "The resulting empowerment will encourage the girls to speak up for their convictions and to assist in the development of programs in their school and their communities."

What's Next?

Kakenya divides her time between her work at the school and fundraising efforts for it. She has many joy-filled moments observing her students practicing algebra, dancing, and singing. They even have fun talking to people in America over the Internet.

Kakenya believes that her school can help make more dreams come true. She explains, "My hope is that when our girls leave to go on to secondary school, they [will] have received a foundation that is as solid as any child's in China, Europe, or America." The parents of Kakenya's students feel this way, too. "When I shared that vision with the girls' parents, a round of applause from them confirmed that this is a shared dream," she says.

Preservation of Culture

Kakenya's school also preserves important cultural and domestic values. Girls learn the life skills of their village. This allows them to carry on family traditions. They also learn about the latest ways to improve their farms, the health of their cows, and their homes. As a result, families feel the immediate benefits of the school—and a girl's education becomes a good investment for everyone.

A Long Journey

It's been a long journey for Kakenya from the days of reluctant parents and elders to the Kakenya Center for Excellence. Kakenya has made her dream come true. Through hard work and determination, she migrated to the United States for the opportunity to attend college and gain valuable knowledge. Now she has returned home to share this knowledge with others. In the process, Kakenya Ntaiya has reshaped her community and redefined herself.

WORDWISE

migration: moving from one part of the world to another

refugee: a person who is forced to leave home because it is too dangerous for him or her there

scholarship: money to help you continue studying

voluntary: something that is done because you want to do it, not because you must do it

On the MOVE!

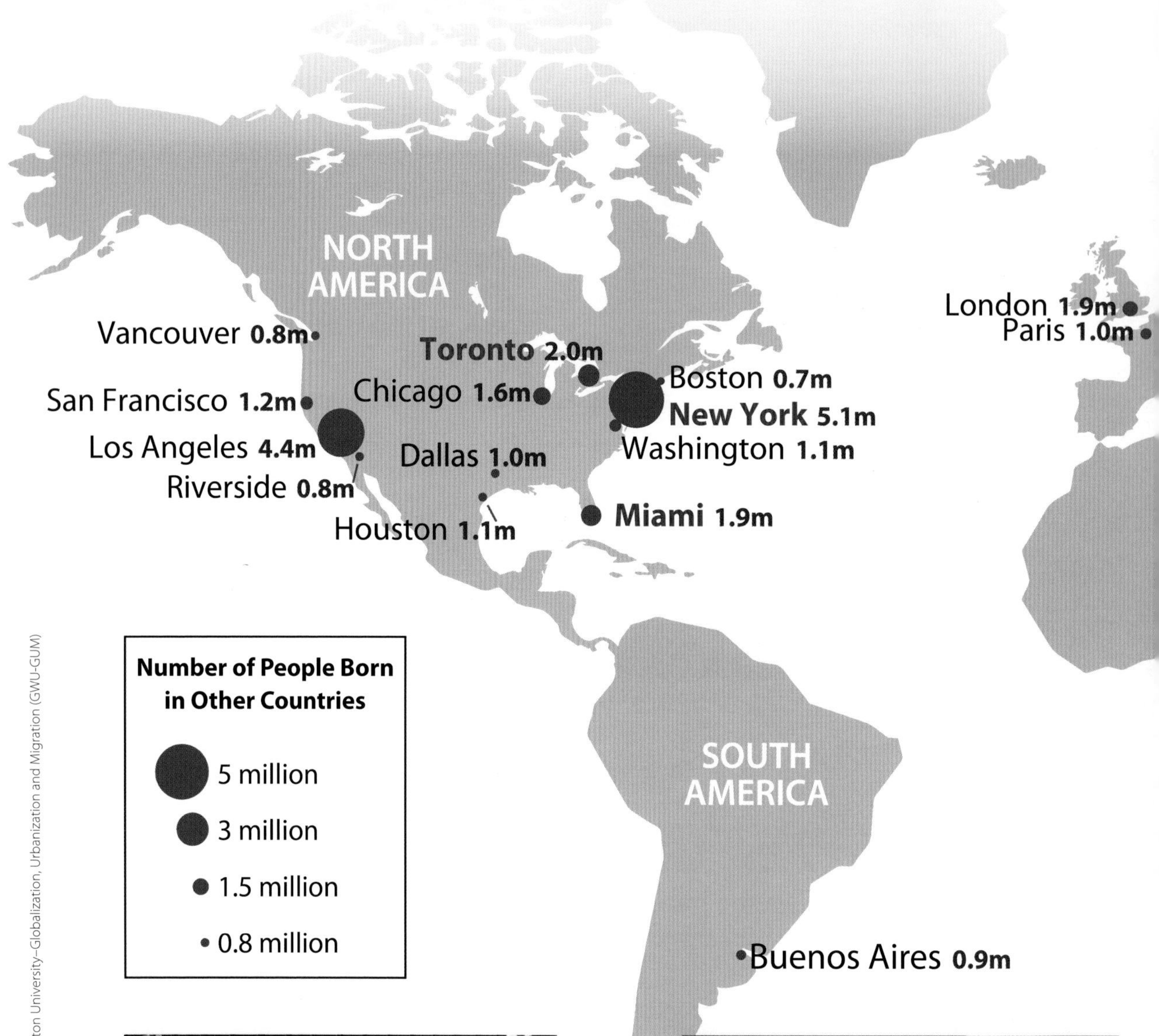

Source: George Washington University–Globalization, Urbanization and Migration (GWU-GUM)

Miami, United States: *Cubans play dominoes in Little Havana. Other newcomers are from Haiti and Jamaica.*

New York, United States: *New York City has the most immigrants anywhere. These new residents make life in New York exciting and diverse.*

MIGRATION HAS GONE GLOBAL. This map of gateway cities around the world shows that there are many migration destinations. People are on the move like never before. Some, like Kakenya Ntaiya, are voluntary migrants in search of opportunity. Others are refugees, seeking a safe place away from war, persecution, or other hardships.

Migration has created incredible diversity. These facts from four gateway cities are evidence that the world has become a global community.

Toronto, Canada: *This shop is in Toronto's Chinatown. Many people come to Toronto from Asian countries like China and India.*

Dubai, United Arab Emirates: *Many workers from India, Pakistan, and Bangladesh find jobs in Dubai. New residents make up a large part of the population there.*

adapted from a report by Brian Reed that aired on NPR's *Morning Edition*, February 16th–17th, 2011

A Sinking Nation Prompts MIGRATION

Natural disasters often strike suddenly and without warning. People must react with little time to think about where to go or what to do. Yet there is a natural disaster happening right now on the islands of Kiribati. Fortunately, it is happening slowly, so the islanders can plan what they must do.

Kiribati (KEER-uh-buhs) is a nation of tiny islands clustered in an area of the Pacific Ocean about twice the size of Alaska. More than 40,000 people live on one island, South Tawara, the capital.

Sitting 2 meters (6.5 feet) above sea level, these islands are worrisome. Why? Many residents think that warmer temperatures and the rising sea are causing the islands to sink.

People see high tides running through the sands and killing crops. They also see the water creeping toward their homes. "The sea level, now it comes to the road, even to the houses," says South Tawara resident, Ata Merang.

In addition, people have noticed extended dry seasons. This can cause water to become scarce.

This young Kiribati resident watches as waves wash into the village.

Migrating with Dignity

Kiribatian President Anote Tong is so concerned about the rising sea levels and other changes that he has put a plan in place to help his citizens. President Tong hopes his plan will give Kiribatian citizens the opportunity to "migrate with dignity."

President Tong thinks his plan will make a difference. "What it means is that we don't just pack up our people from the villages and transport them to one center in Australia and say, 'Ok, there you are,' " he says. Instead, he is trying to find a way for people to move slowly, adapt to their new surroundings, and establish their own communities in other countries.

The first experiment in this kind of migration is the Kiribati Australia Nursing Initiative (KANI). More than 80 students from Kiribati are studying nursing at Australia's Griffith University. Typically, students train and go back home. They then apply their skills to help their developing country. What is different about KANI students is that they might not have a country to go back to.

Living in Another Culture

Tibea Baure is one such student studying nursing in Brisbane, Australia. Moving from a tiny island nation like Kiribati to a suburb outside Brisbane has its challenges. For one thing, it is too quiet. "Not like back on the island. They shout, and they can sing anytime they want to sing," Tibea says. The unfamiliar silence makes her feel lonely.

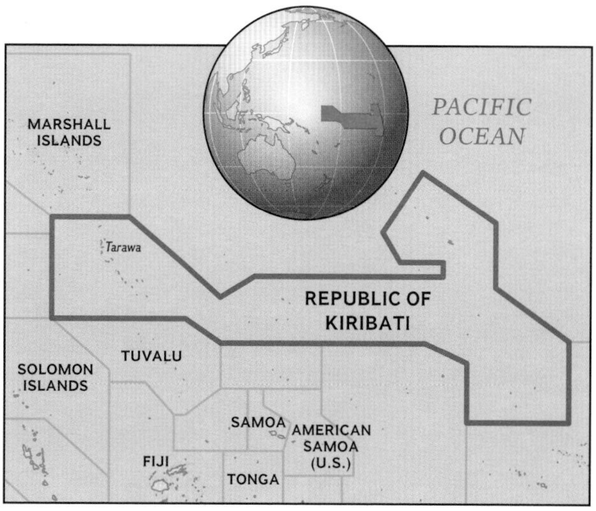

Another friend in the nursing program found it very hard to sleep on a bed at first. Instead, she unrolled the traditional woven mat that she brought with her from the islands. "I have to sleep on the floor!" she announced to her home-stay mother.

Preserving a National Identity

Many of the older residents of Kiribati do not think that the islands are sinking. Although Tibea wants her parents to move to Australia, they don't think that rising water is a threat. What is a threat, many Kiribatians believe, is the loss of their national identity. What will it mean if their country no longer exists? Who will they be?

KANI students have found one answer—a way to maintain their Kiribatian heritage in their new country. They gather every Wednesday night at someone's home, sit on their mats, and sing island songs. In that way, they remember Kiribati and feel just a little bit closer to home.

Moving On

People around the globe are on the move. Answer these questions to join them.

1. What was Kakenya's dream?
2. In order, list the steps Kakenya took to be able to migrate.
3. Kakenya wants to enroll 150 students by 2013 in grades four through eight. Will she achieve this goal? Tell why or why not.
4. Why might people have to leave Kiribati? What is President Tong's plan for this migration?
5. How are Kakenya's and Tibea's experiences similar? How are they different?